Bruce Hale's Magical Experience with
Christopher Johnson

Mary Fallin

Forward: Constance Vincent

Bob young, tyrek young, and Lisa Currie inc.

Co-Writers of Mary Fallin

Constance Vincent
Judy Donnelly
Kayla Hale
Cathrine Price
Mary Fisher
Bob West
Jerry Payne
William Goldman
Lisa Currie
Elaine Adams
Todd Holm
Myra Zarnowski
Michelle Wood
Nicholas Dirks
Karl Marx
Zhao Guoping
Luise Miller
Vivi Holt
Sarah Constantin
Jennifer Tuttle
Becca Givens
Jennifer Wisdom
Kathy Wilson
Alexis Sanchez
Peng Chongqing

Isbn: 978-0-359-83604-8

Newspaper and Freedom press conference
PS: (Quote from John Dewey)

Mazzio's pizza   --- Kellis Robinet , Jema wood
Ponca city stop N go ---Holly Johnson, Richard Allen
Staples --- Dennis Neil , Nathan Wood, Leon Jones
Walgreen ---Johnny Freeman, Robert Myers
Belle Plaine News --- Tim Scotter, Shel Silverman
Rural Messenger --- Alyssa Runyon, Lisa Jackson
Stilly post --- Sally Asher, Sophia Trump
The Saturday evening Post --- Jerry Palyash, James Kushner
Daily Bytes--- Jeni McGee, Perry Lin, Eric Trump
Kansas Hunter ---David Seaton, Samba Xia
Kansas Eagle ---Lance Garrett, Kyle Tork, William Graves
The Ponca city news --- Cody Griesel, David Holt
The Newkirk Herald Journal --- Steven Jobs, Henry Hager
Prairie Connection ----Agnes Nye, Carl Fry, Donald Trump
Stephan Pastis VS Jim Toomey   --- Ina Davis, Amy Storm
Mort Walker and Sherman's Lagoon --- Anderson Cooper, Ke Hu
Courier Traveler --- Frank Eaton, Vahe Gregorvan
Stillwater News press ---Chris Day, Randy Thompson
Boomeran's --- Peter Dixon, William Joyce, Jeff Watts,
Rocky Mountain's candy --- Heather Davis, Mary Clancy
Pizza Hut ---Eric Hill, Abbey Wood, Lucas Wood,

The *FAME* cloud (a quote from John Dewey)

Porch Kathrine Collins Monty Harper Adam Proctor Stephen
Gilpin David King Barbara Hanby William Morrow
Kelsey Lee Annapolis Montuwa Emily Krajicek Steven tucker
Eva Amber Sheila Moore Lisa hicks Shell John Berryman
Deborah Underwood Margaret Laura Mila Pana Attocknio
Poppy Louise Brandi George James Kimbreu Samantha Gillison
Beverly Cleary Karen Shade Peter toy Laura Yirak Eric Smith
Amy Ryan Diane Goettel Roberts Haas sherphard Gamble Daren
Challman Russell Roberts Tana Welch Mike Barbara Ishel
Aaron Norcross Dickinson Jeff Preston Bezos John Bartley
Carrie Lorig Lisa Clap Mackenzie Bezos Mark Willaims
Enchanted Valley shawn Bird princess posey Robert zimmer
Pat quinn sundar pichai l. duane Wilson david smith
elena murphy David holt Hoyt wu sheryln sandburg , Sam Ed
mark zukerburg john chamber, Lottie Evelyn Williams, joe Biden
Jennifer Gates, Zachary Dell, Spencer Trump, Anne Davis
Lisa Currie, Susan Wojcincki, Nicholas Dirks, James Devney
Wu Jing, Peng ChongQing, Wang Guiqiang, Dou Yu**, Cai Ming**

Beverly Cleary

In a tone of Mrs. Qimby
Henry Huggins is a hero
Davy Binney is a character
Children go to school daily,
They grow like Beanstalk
If Ramona Ericson ever wonders
Which is good regardless the elf dancers

David Foldman

He seems a tiny mouse alike
Often he sits still
Until Zuto and Benson join in
Boyscotts and Nilla cookies
Hot Longjing tea and Fresh Strawberry
All items at Kitchen are dreamy
David Adler often recalls tom Edison
The drama of Cam and Sam
The adventure of Jansen and Kat
Colorful life, all natural to Ina Davis and Peter Natti

Kenny Snicely

Under the eye of Phylli's Perry
Amos Brooke comes near
If Nibbles Trapp dares
Fleet Milton would square 5 to make 25 donuts
He hope that Tom Hanks were a pastor

Illinois
New Mexico
Iowa
Mr. Kenny and Mrs. Scurry travel along,
The Fall of Niagara waterfall

---an attraction

Courage and Faith help Fort Atkinson

Lawton and Houston

James Apple,
James Smith,
James Avery,
Why do they support John Dewey?

A wonder for tough staff
Yet we look forward to Helena, Riverside, Tampa, and Topeka
We know the Brownback Selwells,
We know the yellow river sealions,

Disagreement

She says "yes"
He says "wait"
I assume that I need to decide , myself
So I walk off,
It happens that the day is April Fool's day
I post a post about "a mouse has eaten a giant pumpkin"
How many people agree?
How many people will deduce the size of a food?
I leave the answers to readers
How many of you know the answers from this title?!!

Constance Vincent

It is about a diligent Oxen
That plows hard and deep
With some artificial decoration,
The field is rich
The harvest is plump
The sky celebrates with white blanket and orange sunset
Two Reindeer and a giant Yak,
All shadow and all bright moonlight find their peace
The tree branch on upper left looks brushy and curious

Constance Vincent,
Why do you persist Hoyt and Bost the same as Kurtz?
A brown bear is nice
So does a red hen house

Parenting

A baby was born innocent
A pair of parents formed
The feeding is frequent
The cuddling is cozy

Life is magical
First comes love
Next comes marriage
When a baby comes, things are tough

Parenting involves trust, cooperation
Jenny, Melania, Shawn, and Lily just did well

Adult-ish for Vanko

A term for 18 year old or older
A book for open minded eyes
A plant in the view of Cristina and Annapolis

Alice Nebbley --- a Nightingdale

She appears in a novel
Portraited As a Beverly Hill star
She is a bird
That does not twitter
But swim in DiCamillo Lake
Her best friends are Raymie , Roger, Goxhan, Frank, and Kate

Aeshna Zyan-Shawnee

Umbrella
Temper-Storage Cup
Fried dumplings

You give me these to rhyme with
I store the coffee in my poems
I sell my paintings to Moon Flakes

Robert Southey

He makes a Ham Sandwich
He eats Green Eggs
He Swallows Octopus, Raw
He is a master of Shaolin Sonnets---
A poetry form that Paul Negri manages

Yimmer's Ears

Deaf, unless ears,
Vivid, sharp eyes,
Mute, verbal disability,
Blind, vision blurred,
Crippled, need assistance walking

Cherish being ordinary---
No accomplishment
But Slavery Free Settlement

Natalie SnowFlakes

A poet who picks forgotten fruits
A fame reminds us of Sun-Moon lake
A 55-word story composer in Christie Kelly

Andrea Wulf

A shuiling "waterbay" type
A Millard Hopper Free code
Andrea Wulf paints good stories
We learn art, ewcology, nature,
And we find Agricultural tips in Siberia

Syria, Iran, Germany, Fiji, and Cananda

Five lakes
Four seas
They truly means everything and everywhere
Despite the distance between Jupiter and Sun
We do reach many poets ---and
they shine like Starbucks Coffee beans

Kenya, Greence, Yemen, Jiangsu, and South Korea

Despite Barack Obama and J. K. rowling,
We see Robert Frost, Yu Hua, and Catherine Anderson,
International palaces
Poems brew like bubbling breath

Karl Marx and Salin,
Lenin and Vijay Seshadri,
Ted Hughes and James Muphy,
Almost all family members are cheerful about Danmark man

Portland, New Zealand, and Russia

Not yet to visit
But already familiar with Pat Mather Gordon Brown Ceton,
That John Brown seems puzzled of why people look around,
That Frayed Edges might assume Matt Clay otherwise,
Believe it,
Carroll and Thomas always carry faith
Strange waters
They always welcome brave sailors

A Quote of Adam Kurtz

"You made It to
The Luckiest Page in
The Book! This is a good
Sign. "

"Have A Great Day!"

A voice

By instinct
Conscience hits
Sultry meets Husky
Whispers are soft
The message is clear
Murmuring the South Pole Panda
A voice
Always a Wind cross the Window

Walt Whitman and Abdullah Gul

A confession to how
Often having driven away blocked
---not by physical object
But by Mental Temper

Denise Duhamel

An Egypt travelers
Who chooses for Dim Sum
Not only for Saturdays
But also for Wednesdays

Denise Duhamel
A beef eater in Tibert
Who often rides horse
And often picks 5-Inches Foot-Long sandwich in Subway

Lisa Carney

She reads Lynn Kozma
She hosts Late Night movies
And
she holds Seven Children in one single home

Robert Putnam

A silent muse at Blues Clue concert,
Bob Putnam and Crissy Rosenburg set a stage
While Henneberry and Moritz dance---
The space dance steps enlarge,
Some audiences clap,
Mark Zuckerburg joins,
Maxism and Priscilla join,
Todd Burpo joins,
John Sculley leaves,
Tim Armstrong leaves,
Udi Manber stands up,
After Pulling Robert Putnam out,
A shy face turns green

Dennis Woodside

Behind Gen X,
Next to Motorola,
Woodside works on Project Loon,
With a help of Kleiner Perkins,
Intel, Facebook, Clover, Youtube, Twitter,
One by one
Production makes a difference
More or Less
Marissa Mayer,
Patricia Stokes,
Dan Rarner,
Paul Buchheir,
All or each of them generate a number
The Bigbelly has 10x ->->-> 10 Billion

Vinod Khosla

Venture Foodshop, Aldi, Dollar Tree,
Sun Microssystems cofounder
He makes bit
Prolonging Google Inc.
After 1998 --- 2029 web phase
A current Google-sitter in Web zoo 2.0,
He endorses or Kut,
Embraces Twitter and Digg,
Acknowledged "Emerald Sea", "Oracle ",
Whenever you see Sundar Pichai, or Anderson Cooper,
Whenever you read Eric Schmidt, john Green, kay ryan,
You increase your poetic length

Hassan Shelkh Mohamoud

A kind face
Somalia and Graceful Chile
She allows Free Verse impress the audience

Mogens Lykketoft

A bencemark well made
No flag ship but friendship
Bills and Williams fly to Yemen

A Sign For Better Course

No sign is sign
Rouhani and Rasmussen
They tie knots in Tehran and Copenhagen
We do laugh and relax
So do Fredrik, Mary, Joachim, Nick, Madeline, and joyce

Taller and/or Shorter

I won't fall short
Even if Kgalema Motlanthe dalls short
In meeting Helle Thorning Schmidt
For a long time partnership
In World Peace Forum
Shine Abe, Putin, Matt le la pena, Xi Jingping, Trumps,
Pence, Merrel, Thomas, Gansu, Vietnam, Peru, Cuba, etc
…
All seem feel good about others

Amalieberg Palace

Three Waving Hands
Henrik, Hayrunnisa, and Christian,
One Queen with Jorgen Rosenberg
Historical smiles

Donald Reynold and his humorous short stories

Barack Obama, Michael Pence, Alice Walker,
They shout out aloud:
McDonald farm has an ox
The ox often goes "moooo"

Paul ryan, Ryan Haas, Aldous Huxley, Ying Li,
They wonder, secretly
Braums sells ice cream cones,
Nilla often chooses peanut crackers, often laugh too much

A cop Sheriffs a family matter,
Poetry sits on all shelves,
The crisis often Vaperates
Peaceful Smile secures a frontier lane bowling race

Time Differences

6:35am, 12/12/1997
Austin, Texas,
Which is great to Victoria
That is
8:35pm, 12/25/1997, Beijing, p. R. China

As for Glenn Bost, Gloria Washington, Lawrence Grant,
7:25am, Beijing, 5/22/1993,
Is equivalent to 5:25pm, Chicago, ILLinois 5/21/1993
Why does Zedong Mao was born on 12/26/1903?
Why does Frank Eaton was born on 12/28/1909?

10021968
01021968
05221993
12251997
07131961
08132016
07071946
07111946
11081983
05141972
07042000
…..

Free Verse in Haiku form

Senna

The child cries at her breast.
And the mosquito also bites
The sleeping mother

Basho

With ink-stained lips,
The boy leaves his poem
For the cool outdoors

Peter Yarisford (Sabi and Shari style)

Stillness and solitude –
Sinking into stones,
The trill of cicadas

Basho

On a withered branch
A crow has settled.
Nightfall in autumn.

k. d hurley

no money in amy's bank account
she simply works at a hotel restaurant
surviving through water and leftover meals

2019 school calendar

August 19, 18 days from now
a date to meet your school teachers
note books, pencils, new backpacks, textbooks, lunch money,
all made possible to think

do a good shopping list
go preparing for a school of award winning

poems

if thomas perez agree
he may pay attention to his old sister
judith, billy collins, tom mcdaniel, susan wojcincki,
they all bake "awesome poems"

a "tang" poem can be seen,
a "free verse" can be great,
jennifer ferguson, max barry, bill hslam, tyler buffett,
donnell farris, yan ji, edwin, james devinney, jackie....

Jinks

In some raged place
curious poets fell asleep
Milkyway sky in my palm

My question

Season's Greetings,
what do you eat during 2018 Holiday season,
Green beans?
mashed potatoes?
baked fish?
ham or green peppers?

food,
my favorite subject?
poetry,
my favorite writing

Humor and fun on small mind

pretty girls
ronan and kai
they wonder about nature and ask why?

green hills
an animal stands near
arabella and rose
they smell fresh air ..cheer

afternoon tea
a cup of milk plus a slice of french bread
joseph, theodore, madison, milos, tristan, joseph, joy,
spencer, chloe, and villency, markshen, tyler, sam, tom,
all seem shy

Copan residence

a stranger to banana
joann craft
a fresh design for anne perry

warm april days
christina and vikki piety
they sit, pray for Ken Piety

Ameliawood Yarisford loves to learn

Schooling is cool
we improve, go up,
hands up for a answers from our heart

Back home
we ride on yellow bus
we do scootering

questions and curiosity
all open for a family of children and teachers
kids can do well if parents or teachers pay attention

American Airline / Delta Airline

bright red, dark green,
long sleeves, short skirt,
we walk with wind
we talk without minding others

when we travel
we sit in a flying planet
where only a limited space is available
and we become tense without loosing our temper

Disney Movies

Jurassic Park movie
an adventure for young and cute kids
Haiku turns into a dino

the lost world
wilderness and dinowoods in screen
innocent eyes and tears

green and tall monster
they stalk at Gabi desert in Alaska
scurrying small London Rexuts

Confidence grows with Federle and Hagy , or Vanko

family, friends, relatives,
poems, lyrics, haiku,
texas, illinois, new jersey,
father, sons, daughter, mother,
dancing footsteps
we image magic and romance
a fate is not decided yet revolving around
the alan eagle and briana blair spirits are in
we added joy
we added sunshine
we hide in a shadowy place to escape snowfalls
we agree that poetry prevails

tang poems are very famous all over the world,
one is Yang Juyuan, (steven chen), *杨巨源*

the well know poem he has written is

城东早春

唐代：杨巨源

诗家清景在新春，绿柳才黄半未匀。
若待上林花似锦，出门俱是看花人。

 shijia xinjing zai xinchun, lu liu caihuang ban weiyun
luodai shanglin huashijing, chumen jushi kanhuaren

杨巨源(宋代名将) 百度百科

2019年2月27日 - *杨巨源*约1176—
1207年),字子渊,利州昭化(今四川省广元西南)人,祖籍在成都。享年三十一岁...

english meaning

a poet is refreshed in the morning , green willows and yellow daisy mix
if one wishes to see flowers all over the garden, then get out and join the crowds

Emily Krajicek

knowing is well
knowing another wisdom is better
learning from others could be of best experiences

a missed bus ride
a memory that evokes small lost
a stay-on-track tip could keep one running through dark tunnels

darkness, discouragement, cruelty, confusion, misunderstanding,
all terms could bring in wonder:
why do you care?

we do choose wise terminology
we do choose elegant lotus roots and peals
we do choose tall glass instead of shortcoming

never shrug to escape, but shrug to research and join a platform

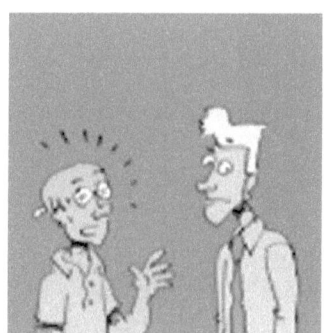
William Pitt and Ebriss Titi

blogging from a to z in april, A is for Abbey Art,
 Z is for Zuomin Zebra, J is for Jingle Poetry,
A is for Shen Clothing Fashion,
 L is for Leonard Murphy business,
T is for Toms shoes, N is for Nick
Lantz, M is for Michael Walsh,
E is for Eric Schmidt,
 P is for Peggy Helmrich,
H is for Hudson fisher,
K is for Kyle Richardson Schmidly,

Friday My Town Shoot Out

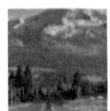

Not many Link Up Today
which is set by Tom L. Wu

Amelia's Dessert

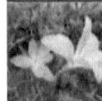

CHEERS TO THE NEW YEAR 2018
which is set by Amelia Wilson

OctPoWriMo 2014

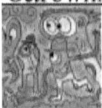

Continuing the Poetry Journey
which is set by Anne Wojcicki

My Memory Art

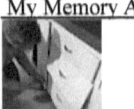

Fixer-Upper
which is set by abbey wood

dVerse
Chijitsu: Lingering Day–dVerse Haibun Monday
which is set by Nina Wise, Sheila moore, and Bruno Wu

Poets United
BLOG OF THE WEEK - AN UPDATE WITH PAUL ANDREW RUSSELL
which is set by Robert myers, Tan Zhikang and Michelle Manser

Magical Mystical Teacher
Ruby Tuesday Too: Eatery Ahead
which is set by Sheng wu and Lawrence Grant

Sunday's Whirligig
Whirligig 157
which is set by Julia Barnes and Keith Edwards

Poetry & Story Inn by Colin Yaccarino at Loyola Pagewell
which is set by Colin Yaccarino and Fallin Page-Bricker

Flash Friday 55 word story by G-man
Sunday 160 syllabus by Monkey Man
Thursday Poets Rally , free verse, Jingle Yan

《山村》这首诗不是唐诗，是宋朝诗人邵雍所写，原文如下：

mountain village, a poem by shaoyong 邵雍

一去二三里，烟村四五家，
亭台六七座，八九十枝花。

one or two miles long in a jiff,
four or five homes from Yunnan village sit near
next to the road, i see six or seven pavilions,
and eight nine ten bunches of flowers

整首诗意思是：

我到外面游玩，不知不觉离家已有两、三里地，
看到不远处的小村庄里，有四、五户人家已经
冒起了炊烟。我信步走去，又看到路边有六、七处
精美的亭阁楼台，独自静静观赏，才发现身边的
树枝上挂着……八朵、九朵，十朵花，真是赏心悦目！

it is a pleasant joy to go outside, observing around,
i count 1 2 3 miles, 4 5 homes, 6 7 pavilions, 8 9 10 flowers
nature is calm and beautiful
I fall silent, admiring the heavenly scene

check out these, we promote world peace
through Jingle Poetry @olive Garden

year 8, may of 2019, Sasha James Maxium bost Philpark, jingle yan,
year 7, may of 2018, stephan peter carl victor Hudson, Ina Davis,
year 6, may of 2017, stephan peter carl victor Hudson, infamous mountain,
year 5, may of 2016, michelle ivana yunaska theilfing Obama, benny wu,
year 4, may of 2015, larry hasty wendy stanley wojcicki, larry page,
year 3, may of 2014, jingle poetry @olive garden administrative, Venetian Peng
year 2, may of 2013, Larry Hasty Wendy Stanley wojcicki, chloe wojin,
year 1, may of 2012, Taylor kong Boomer, Jingle yan, Ted Hills,

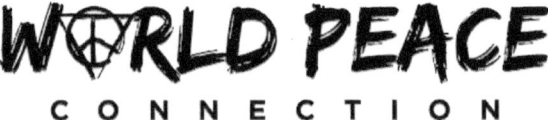

WORLD PEACE
C O N N E C T I O N

why reading poetry makes peace?
how writing poetry can help improving our peace manner?
it is because we care about our mood
and we care about our influences

Vanessa writes some,
Alison writes some,
Jennifer writes some,
Olivia writes some

I feel good when I know my friends having production
I feel good if I am read by a president
I feel flattered if my children read my books
world peace begins with a short verse

Another "Tang" poem

胜亚 . 向群 (Ameliawood Yarisford)
tang poem by ameliawood yarisford

百度糯米网
网页**唐诗胜**
胜利**腾讯年**
年画贺龙眼

baidu nuomi wang,
wang ye tangshisheng,
shengli tengxunnian,
nianhua helongyan

english translation

the baidu search engine is busy as piled sweet rice
a web page that is filled with "tang" poems wins
a victory tengxun year
greeting cards and new year calendars uplift one's spirit in the eye

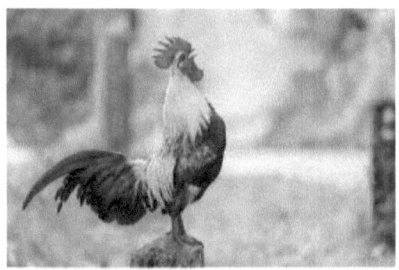

Handsome rooster

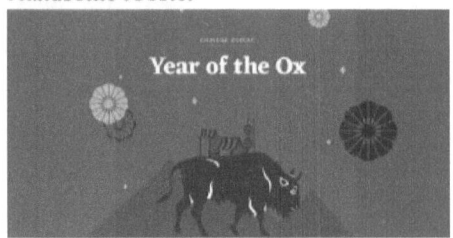

Ox years include 1985, !997, 2009, 2021, 2033, 2045, 2057

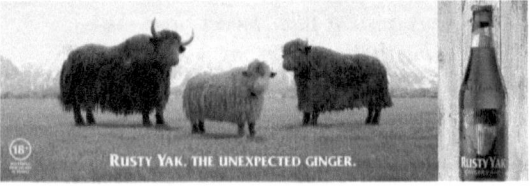

Yak, Jim Henson favorite animal from Tibert Mountain